The Warrior Sings

To Leonarda,
   Thank you so much
for your support.
   From one 'writer' to
another (own it).
      ♡ Michelle

The Warrior Sings

Michelle Dosanjh-Johal

RESOURCE *Publications* · Eugene, Oregon

THE WARRIOR SINGS

Resource Publications
An Imprint of Wipf and Stock Publishers
199 W. 8th Ave., Suite 3
Eugene, OR 97401

www.wipfandstock.com

PAPERBACK ISBN: 978-1-6667-4580-1
HARDCOVER ISBN: 978-1-6667-4581-8
EBOOK ISBN: 978-1-6667-4582-5

07/19/22

Contents

Songs of Love

Songs of Strength

The Warrior Sings

The most beautiful song
echoed in the wintry halls
of the prison
calling attention
to the Angel
in the cold cell,
his wings chained
and bleeding.

"You fool,"
said the prison guard,
"you are cold,
and decrepit, and a
fraction of your former self.
Your wings are chained and bleeding.
Why do you sing?"
The Angel merely smiled
and said, "because, in Love I rise."

So he sang once again,
and the tune echoed
through the wintry hilltops

and barren land
where hope had been lost . . .
A nomad heard it
and came to the cell window.
He saw the chained Angel
and said, "Fool, you are
worse off than me.
Why do you sing?"
"Because, my darling,
in Love I rise."

Days passed
and the Angel continued
to sing.
One day, the prison guard
brought his little girl
and told her to stay put.
Of course, this little girl
seldom did as she was told.
She stole a set of keys and
went exploring when she heard
the most glorious of songs.
She followed the song to the cell
with the Angel.
She opened the cell,
and was overwhelmed with joy and love.

She kissed the Angel on the forehead,

unlocked his chains,

and said "I love you . . ."

And the Angel smiled, and rose.

Surrender

In sorrow, she danced with suffering,
slowly to a savage tune.
Painful pirouettes of pity,
maniacal melodies beneath the moon.

Dancing in the darkened alley,
screaming songs to feed the beast,
kissing suffering's savage lips,
pensively praying for a priest.

Prayers falling upon deaf ears,
suffering silently slits her throat,
bleeding upon the blazing flames,
until there was nothing left to emote.

Her and suffering had become one,
she wore suffering as her skin,
fleshly pains were all but done,
fleshly pleasures were but remiss . . .

The flames no longer could touch her flesh,
they had already devoured everything,

the blood had drained, every ounce . . .
now she rose with darkened wings.

Now she danced a different tune,
whilst others watched and all but wondered,
whispering, wondering, curiously chattering
about this glorious spell that she was under.

Metamorphosis is magic
when darkness merges with the light . . .
rising, rising, our daunting dancer
surrendered serenely to the fight.

Wildest of Storms

If you can sing and dance
in the wildest of storms . . .
If you can love yourself
when darkness is born,
If you can laugh at the night
because you see the stars . . .
Darling, that is just
what you are.

If you can hold yourself
while on your knees,
With salted tears
and bloody pleas.
If your screams can echo
like music in the night,
Darling, I promise . . .
you'll be alright.

So sing, and laugh,
and dance in the storm . . .
So cry, and scream, let your
soul be reborn.

For without the darkness,
stars can't exist . . .
And without love . . .
life is amiss.

Kiss Freedom

Live like your life
is on the line.
Be a
renegade.
Dare
to walk out of the lines.
Dare
to draw your own.
Dare
to live
your own kind of truth.

Fuck their gossip.
Be you anyway.
Love like it's air,
Laugh like the joke
is never ending,
Dance like
it's your last dance.

Hold his hand,
or hers . . .

Let your heart crack
if it lets the light in.
Wear your hair down
and unleash
the wild in your soul.
Burn and
kiss freedom.

Gypsy Dancer

She sings a symphony of somber songs,
a chorus of chaotic screams . . .
She whispers serene promises
amidst the mystery of a dream . . .

Curiosity will confuse her night,
morning dew drips from her breath.
Alas, the river flows into emptiness,
another day that feels like death.

She's riding the waves of oblivion
consumed by flames of chaos,
searching, searching, a gypsy dancer,
opening multiple locks . . .

Exploring the darkest of terrains,
and never finding answers . . .
For the very essence of what she searches
is inside this gypsy dancer . . .

Inside the heart of sorrows,
where time no longer flows,

humanity meets divinity
suffering, it slows.

Inside the whispers of the soul
where solace makes a sound . . .
You will find your answers here,
where hope and love are found.

Kissing the Light

Escape into the abyss of freedom,
surrender the perils of night . . .
Sliced by shards of suffering,
souls prepare to take flight . . .

Feed off the scarcest crumbs
sleep in the darkest night,
vultures are close and hovering
but souls will rise to new heights.

Bleeding hearts will succumb
and surrender into the fight.
Pain and darkness pulverizing
and finally kissing the light.

Beautiful Suffering

My world was darkened,
my eyes were bold,
my lens was black,
my soul was cold . . .
Ashes flew
in the dark angel's grasp
darkened entities
unleashed their wrath.
Until I became the fire
became the breath
universal pulse,
humanity took death.
I burned completely,
I lost my name . . .
my essence emerged
from the flames.
I changed my sight,
I felt new wings,
changed the game
in beautiful suffering.

Light The Fire

Light the fire
and watch me burn
let the masses
take their turn.
Put the dagger
in my back,
allow the blood
to flow through cracks . . .

Let your cold breath
freeze my soul,
with wavering tongues
lies will be told.
Allow the fire to
turn to ashes
let me suffer
one thousand lashes.

Anguish and angst
bone fatigue
fists that bruise . . .
silent screams.

Let the silence
mask my pain,
let suffering
speak my name.
Fire, blood
ashes and ice.
Watch me perish
then watch me rise.
Amidst the screams
the anguish dies
transforming fear
into a Heavenly high.

Strength

Strength isn't always the

mighty fist or jagged sword . . .

Sometimes she's a gentle whisper . . .

The voice whispering in the darkness . . .

Softly nudging your spirit . . .

You can do this . . .

You can do this . . .

You will do this.

It is what it is.

Accept,

Step into it,

Surrender.

Do not resist the darkness.

Love anyway,

Despite the flaws

of life

of men

of humanity

of self . . .

Love anyway

swim in the suffering

and one day

just as the sun surely peaks

you will rise again.

I Will Put on Red Lipstick

—inspired by Amanda Lovelace's *red lipstick poetry*

There will come a day
I will put on red lipstick
for these lips
were meant to be
bold,
just like the voice
inside.
And the child
who held dreams
in her eyes
will laugh again.
The woman who wept
will float on
wings of love . . .
Because on that day
I will grow wings
to fly.

Apologize

I use to apologize
for everything.
I use to apologize
in the fear
that my presence
somehow burdened
your peace.
I use to apologize
for being.
I use to apologize
for breathing.
Then it dawned on me
that my presence was
just as worthy as
yours,
my breath was sovereign
my soul was free.
My being was no less worthy
than the celebrity you worship
for love is my crown
that takes space
unapologetically . . .

So
I won't fucking apologize
anymore.

Rise Like an Angel

If they try
to throw you
in the flames,
let them . . .
and transcend
in the fire,
darling . . .
show them
you are magic,
show them
love transcends all,
show them
your divinity
and rise
like an Angel.

Dance Despite the Pain

Dance despite the pain
laugh anyways
let love win
manufacture joy
smile though your heart
is breaking
and one day
the joy will become real
and light will shine again.

Fly in Freedom

Though my heart may be broken
in a thousand pieces,
I am not a victim.
I am a warrior.
My poetry is my battle cry.
My writing is a call for hope
and for dreams
to never give up
despite the songs that sorrow will sing.

Though it may be dark
in this cave
I revel in the knowledge
that it is a cocoon
that stimulates the
growth of my wings
so one day
I can fly
in freedom.

Bathe With Me

My tears drop into the universal pool which leads to the ocean
of healing waters . . . will you bathe with me there?
Will you allow your soul to be raw . . . naked . . . vulnerable . . .
if only for a moment . . .
Will you step out of the illusion, if only for a breath?
Will you baptize yourself with your own healing?
Become reborn?
And bathe with me there?
In the waters of truth, of wisdom, of divinity?
Cry with me then . . . and let suffering be your guide
to your light, and your humanity be your guide
to your divinity.

Ultimate Paradox

Celebrating the light is easy . . .
But how does one embrace the light
without knowing the darkness?
For, without it, there can be no light.
Without pain, we could not deepen our joy.
Without the cold, we could not appreciate the sun.
And without sadness,
we could not deepen our moments of gratitude.

The irony lies then
in the beauty of the darkness,
the beauty of the suffering,
for life is inundated
with paradoxes.
The storms which tear down the trees
help to rebuild the earth.
The sun which burns you
gives us life . . .
and someone who you love
so deeply
can completely shatter your heart.
The ultimate paradox:

Beautiful suffering
which helps us to truly
worship the light
within us all.

The Candle

How does she
rise above the
damned who have made
darkness their dance?

How does she
see through
shadows that shiver
in sacrifice sublime?

How to hear
beyond the shrieks
and screams
that echo
through hollow homes?

How do haunted hearts
find their haven?

To see, to breathe?
To feel, to be?

To rise, to fly
beyond blackened skies?

One simple candle
one simple flame
one small kindness
one simple name
emitted from the breath
escaping from her lips
fragments
melded magically
into a rebirth.

It was her all along.
It was her all along.
It was always her.

The Candle.

Freedom

The chains lay broken
piled upon the ground
crumbled into bits . . .
and she rose
with wings too tired to fly
and songs to sorrowful to sing . . .
but she rose anyway.

She noticed that some of the chains
had become embedded
in her shoulders,
weighing her soul
and tiring her spirit . . .
but she rose,
and carried the remnants as her own
and that was what mattered.

She learned freedom came
with a hefty price . . .
acceptance
surrender
left resistance in the broken chains

lying upon the ground,

pieces in her shoulders . . .

the ghosts of their anguish

would haunt with reverberating echoes

reaching the soul . . .

but she rose,

she smiled,

and she loved.

Phoenix

My grandma use to call me *soni chiree* . . .
she didn't realize I was actually a phoenix
born again
and again
and again
from the fires of transformation.

Perhaps I am a Greek reincarnation then
of Hestia
Goddess of fire and sacrifice
now just an Indian peasant
embodying divinity,
a divine peasant
who happened to luck into
a life of education and freedom
but also
unlucky in suffering.
I am more,
and I am less . . .
Human
and divine.

What does it matter?

Don't you know

souls all come

from the same fire, just different flames

like the same ocean

carries different waves

and such are the flames of sacrifice

all consuming

all connecting

all transforming . . .

and this is the very fire

of the phoenix

that is in me,

it is also in you.

You just haven't realized it yet.

I Blazed

Soul naked, I blazed
through the wintry storm
fires of my heart
keeping me warm . . .
soles of feet
upon earth and ice,
kissing the darkness
with wandering eyes.

Lost, abandoned,
broken but free.
Which path to take?
Who will I be?
Fires of my heart
keeping me warm.
Soul naked, I blazed
through the wintry storm.

What is this fire
calling to me?
Burning these chains
and setting me free . . .

Alchemized in power
as self love takes form.
Soul naked, I blazed
through the wintry storm.

I Declare

I declare . . .
I declare
the strength of the ocean
and cleansing healing waters of the sea.

I declare . . .
I declare
the ferocity of the fire
and the passion of the flames.

I declare . . .
I declare the nurturing cultivation
of mother Earth . . .
sturdy, fertile, ready to prosper.

I declare . . .
I declare the tenacity
of the midnight sky
and the resilience of her lessons.

I declare . . .
I declare the vitality

of the sun
and the mercy of her rays.

I declare strength, healing, ferocity,
passion, nurturing, resilience, vitality, and
mercy.
I declare the power
of Love.
I declare.

Howl at the Moon

Howl at the moon,
dance in the night.
Alchemize the darkness,
become the light.

Ignite the flames,
dance in the fire.
Laugh at the pain,
allow it to inspire.

Dance in the rainstorm,
chant pagan songs.
Absorb ancient wisdom,
let Love hold you strong.

Howl at the moon,
ignite the flames.
Alchemize the darkness,
speak Love's name.

Breathe and Just Be

I've seen sights
that can't be unseen
heard dark songs
that bless the deaf.
Entered a nightmare
that mocked every dream.
Danced with demons
that have stolen my breath.

Sometimes I've raged,
Sometimes I've cried.
Sometimes I've sinned,
Sometimes I've lied.
I am the Angel,
I am the Devil.
I am divinity yet
I am darkness disheveled.

When I quiet the chaos,
I let go the rage,
I atone for the sin
amidst smoke and sage.

Then my soul speaks
in mesmerizing tones.
I may be weary,
but I'm never alone.

I sing new songs
as I kneel and confess,
touch aching souls
that warrant caress.
See with new eyes,
conjure new dreams,
dance with the Angels,
breathe and just be.

Rage Against the Night

Don't hide to make them comfortable.
Don't shrink to please them.
Don't dim your shine
to please the world.

Burn your flame bright.
Rage against the night.
Honor your light.

Destroy old paradigms.
Shift views that confine you,
burn the box.
Breathe and sigh.
Sit and rest, live and love,
dance, laugh and fly.

Tell Me to Speak

They tape my mouth
and tell me to speak . . .
Sew my eyes shut
and tell me to see.
Put me in darkness
and ask me to seek.
Put me in water
and tell me to breathe.

What is this game
where I can't seem to win?
What is this game,
I don't want to begin.
But here I am
against my knowing,
no words, only darkness,
raging waters flowing.

They tape my mouth
and tell me to speak . . .
Sew my eyes shut
and tell me to see.

Put me in darkness
and ask me to seek.
Put me in water
and tell me to breathe.

So I changed the game,
I tore off the tape.
Cut open the thread,
and put on a cape.
I learned how to swim,
found my own light . . .
I can speak, I can see,
I can breathe, I can fly.

Do Not Weep at Winter's Wiles

The wildest wind storm whispered my name
whilst cherry blossoms danced amidst the rain
into the waters that called from the wild,
whilst embracing my innermost child.

What is this phenomenon calling to me?
What is this force that can not be seen?
What is this struggle, what is this dance?
What is this music, a hypnotic trance?

It beckons in benevolence, it sings songs sublime.
It moves with magnificence, tantalizing time.
It heals hallowed hearts, it mends maddened minds.
It unearths the secrets that serenity sighs.

So do not weep at winter's wiles,
let the wayward forces run wild.
Let the flame rage, transform in the fire,
let your soul soar and the storm lift you higher.

Victim or Victor

Will you fall
or will you rise?
Is it your victory
or your demise?

Reality is a
fragile thing . . .
Perspective skews
songs that you sing.

The web is deceitful.
The veil is a lie.
Time is illusion
as are good byes.

So control the flame
lest it burn you . . .
Victim or victor,
What do you choose?

No Match

I've been to Hell,
now resting in purgatory
I've walked with feet of softness
into the flames
shielded myself with kindness
in the piercing heat
lighting my way with love
amidst darkness.

I've been to Hell
singing songs of Angels
amidst the devil's lair
whilst demons' screams
pierced the air.
Whilst eagles cried
and plucked my eyes . . .
I held the vision in my heart.

So hold on,
kiss the ground with your feet,
walk slowly against defeat,
let love in and attach

to your purpose.
The kiss of Judas,
Spirit of Apate
Seduction of Peitho
will be no match.

Still She Grew

First she was buried
in grief so deep
she almost forgot her name.
But she knew.
Then came
the storm
that almost broke her . . .
almost, not quite,
still she grew.
Even when the sun
scorched her body
with heat from
the flames of Hell . . .
still she grew.
And one day
everyone gasped
at what she had always
known to be true . . .
she was a rose
and she was beautiful.

Fragrance of the Rose

Can you sit in darkness
whilst searching for the light?
Succumb to savage suffering
and surrender before the fight?

Can you swim the oceans
whilst sirens songs are born?
Can you smell the fragrance of the rose
though bleeding from the thorns?

For every dark night has its stars,
every suffering offers wisdom.
Even sirens sing a seemly song,
even love will have its victims.

But there is magic in the stardust,
salvation in surrender's songs.
For the fragrance of the rose soothes
every broken heart done wrong.

Become Anointed

I was a whisper
until I became the thunder,
all that didn't serve me
was torn asunder.

I was a breeze
until I became the storm,
all that was weak
was made to transform.

I was sitting in darkness
so I became the fire.
Alchemized the darkness
with the flames of desire.

I was feeble prey
until I became the lion.
Broke rules that don't serve me,
ignorance defying.

I was a servant,
but decided to be Queen.

I was invisible,
but now I am seen.

So come sit with me,
you won't be disappointed.
Love is a magic potion,
become anointed.

The River Runs Deep

The raging river
called my name,
deeming my whole world
trivial.

She tamed my
Chaos,
she kissed my face
reminding me of all
things pluvial.

She whispered
witch secrets,
beckoned the spirits,
reminded me
to step in
sovereignty.

She healed my woes
and washed my sins,
and rose me up

into
my divinity.

Listen then,
to the call
of the wild
to the secrets
Mother Nature
keeps.

The keeper
of wisdom,
the healer of
heartaches,
in the place where
the river
runs deep.

She Sings Me a Lullaby

She sings me a lullaby
at the river's edge
whispering the wisdom
of the ancients
breathing the
benediction of the breeze
baptized in brooks
of benevolence.
Wading
in the waters
that weep.
Waking to
the truth
we seek.
Wading.
Waking.
Wading.
Waking.
Free.

Look Into Your Heart

She fills the void
with diamonds and pearls . . .
hoping their shimmer
will rub off
on the ache in her soul . . .
but to no avail.

He fills the emptiness
with salacious passions . . .
hoping this will
be the one
that feels like home . . .
but fails.

They bury themselves
in work and pleasure . . .
thinking this will
make them forget
darkness and dejection . . .
life assails.

For
blind are the greedy,
aching are the lustful,
cogs in a system,
mad and meaningless,
forever waiting
for their ship to sail.

Halt, and listen.
Halt, and be . . .
The ship
is the destination,
life is the sea . . .
The treasure
was always within
your reach.
Look into your heart,
and finally see.

Blazing in a Blue Fire

Alchemized in the depths of sorrow,
healing through the flames of love,
kissing hope on the dawn of tomorrow . . .
rising to the faith above.
Oh healing flames the
Angels sire . . .
Blazing in a blue fire.

I am the light
I am the storm
I am the fire
I am reborn.
For in the flames
I will rise higher
Blazing in a blue fire.

Oh the melodies
the Angels sing,
after sufferings
the world will bring.
Ego left in the funeral pyre
Blazing in a blue fire.

See through eyes they cannot see
feel the truth they cannot be
immerse yourself in love and light
set ablaze before the night
be the love your soul desires,
Blazing in the blue fire.

I Rise in Fire

I use to be fire
until they watered me down,
told me who I could and couldn't be.
Told me what I could and couldn't see,
and I listened.

I use to be fire
until they took away my air,
told me girls were mild and meek,
women were soft and weak,
not fire.
and I listened.

I use to be fire
until they reduced me to my looks,
and said my value was in my ability
to please others
through self sacrifice.
and I listened.

I'm done listening.

Now I'm talking.

I'm feeding my fire

with soul food . . .

Fanning the flames

with the breeze of benevolence . . .

adding the fuel

of self love . . .

And my flames are growing

out of control

unquenchable

in love

lighting the path

for all who stand with me

because

as

I rise in fire,

so does everyone

surrounding me.

There is No Such Thing as too Much Fire

There is no such thing as too much fire . . .
My muse woke me
with fire
whilst I lay dying
now the flames burn
embers no more
and I am alive
I am alive.

There is no such thing as too much desire . . .
My muse lifts me
in passion
with butterfly wings
and heart strings
and Angels sing
divine songs
and I thrive
I thrive.

There is no such thing as too much love . . .
My muse kissed me
with phantom lips

and now her love lifts me

higher and higher

into the planes

of the ethereal

and I strive

I strive.

Because . . .

There is no such thing as too much fire.

I Persist

I chased against winter
as she laughed
with her icy breath . . .
so instead
I stopped racing
and I gave her a kiss.

Darkness grabbed me
and tried to suffocate me
with his limbs . . .
so instead
I danced with him
and it was bliss.

Fire surrounded me
and trapped me
with her blaze
so instead
I burned in surrender,
I couldn't resist.

Then magic happened
amidst frozen lips,
while dancing in chaos
my soul lit and ripped . . .
I surrendered,
I transformed,
I persist . . .
I persist.

Burn

I want to dance.
I want to move
to the beat
of a quintessential symphony
and get lost in the music
of existence.

I want to sing.
I want to sing softly
and I want to sing bold
so that the echoes resound
and reverberate in creation
and my essence reborn
can never be silenced again.

I want to see.
I want to open my eyes
anew to the magic in
the snowflakes,
the same magic
that flows in love
light

and
sets my soul free.

I want to breathe.
I want to fill my lungs
expansive with air
and my soul with life
my lungs
bursting in passion
and fire.

I want to burn.
I want to take all my pain
every ounce of my suffering
and light a match
and feel the fucking burn
until I am reduced to ashes
and nothing, nothing, nothing
could ever hurt me anymore.

Then I will rise.
Then I will laugh.
Then I will breathe, I will see
and dance
and sing.
Then I will be reborn . . .
but first, first, first
I must burn.

First I Must Rage

Sometimes I rage
sometimes I burn
and my screams echo through the hollow caves of hell
and return right back to pierce my soul.

Still I will scream.
Still I will rage.
Still I will burn
until I transmute in the flames
and transform the anger
into pain
into grief
into sorrow so deep
it will weep
upon a seed of hope
and water this hope
with my tears of sadness
and sprinkle a dash of love . . .
Only then
can the seed grow
into something
magical.

But first,

first I must rage.

She Found Herself a Dream

She took the strands of pain
and wove them into
a delicate tapestry of words
to wear around her
fragile heart . . .
infused with the magic
of love,
she wore her emotive cape
of poetry
and flew
to starry skies
where dreams rise,
and found herself
a dream
or two.

The Breath Before the Kiss

A myriad of dreams
amalgamate before
the deepest darkness.

Deep breath in,
deep breath out,
pulsations of life
within my body.

Like the breath before the kiss . . .
the night before the dawn
is a mystical occurrence . . .
the duck before the swan.

Cursed or blessed?
The mud, the seeds
of suffering
without which
there could be no lotus.

Cursed or blessed?
The dark cocoon

devoid of light
without which
new wings could not
be born.

So be born again
my love.
Breathe in the night air
before you kiss the dawn.
Wrap your wings around you,
be the butterfly
or the swan . . .

Rise.
Rise.
Rise.
Thrice into
your power.

Loose Ends

Loose ends are messy
like the shaking hands
holding the frayed rope
wondering whether to tie
the noose into
a knot that was neat.

She was dead anyway
dead
of passion, hope,
devoid of life.
Messy loose ends
were all that she had left
to stare at.

But strange morning whims
infiltrate
with the aroma of coffee
and the sights
of cinnamon sprinkled
on drab morning toast
stirrings of hunger

quenching of thirst

and so

with the first light of dawn

whispers of solace

urge

the deadened heart

to beat again.

Beat by beat by beat . . .

She feels her

heart beat,

as she breathes

again

tying the loose ends

this time onto an

anchor

called hope.

Slay

You can't escape the beast,
you must face it and feel his wrath . . .
then slay.
You can't escape the fire
you must burn and transform,
then pray.
When your tears create an ocean
you mustn't drown,
swim.
When your voice is silenced,
sing your sorrows softly
in a hymn.

For every beast
can be slayed,
fire transforms
if we pray.
Every tear
can heal the soul . . .
Every voice is strong,
every soul is bold . . .

Sing,
Swim,
Heal
Begin . . .
Alchemize
Pray
and slay.

Wash My Sorrows

I am the confined
locked in a prison
crafted by my own psyche
deliriously raging
at the woman in the mirror
to set me free.

I am the blind
endlessly reaching
for treasures and jewels
glittering magic
which appear far
in the distance;
oh, how far
my soul has strayed.

I am the fool
searching for love
evaded by the frenzy
of passionate idolization
searching, in vain

for something

that was always within.

I am the confined,

I am the blind,

I am the fool,

I am deprived . . .

I am lost

yet I am found.

I am the pulse

where freedom sounds . . .

Only I can wash

my sorrows in the waters

of my own soul.

Rain on Me

Regrets are like raindrops
eroding the foundation
of your home.
If you're not careful
regrets will become
the storm in which
you lose yourself.
Regret is opposite
of acceptance then.
A killer of
gratitude, delivering
deviant darkness,
emanating vibrations
of crimson shadows.
For storms
and darkness are meant
to serve the light,
not deify darkness . . .

Rain on me then,
drench my soul
in sorrow so deep,

joy must elude me

for this moment.

Rain on me then

and quench

my insatiable thirst

for passion

and a desire

to be seen . . .

as invisibility cloaks me

my vision skewed

by the murky waters,

my essence

emanating in emptiness

the hollow hearts

in which seeds are

harrowed.

Rain on me then,

in the place that hope

habituates

water these seeds

of self compassion . . .

allow

understanding

to flourish

into soul purpose

and love.

Just don't get stuck
in the storm my love and
whatever you decide . . .
Never never never
regret love.

It's Time

It's time.
It's time to start a revolution . . .
Discard your old skin
and allow your wings to unfold.

It's time.
It's time to dance in the rain
and rejoice
in the lessons
the storms have taught you.

It's time.
It's time to rise out of the shadows
and allow the sunshine
to dance across your face
and penetrate
your soul.

It's time.
It's time to be born again.
Reborn in the fire,
alchemized in its blaze,

forged into freedom.

Stop playing small

and start your revolution.

Songs of Gender

Within the Broken Pieces

I was the perfect
Indian bride.
I ate up all the falsehoods
like ladoos on my wedding day.
I welcomed the lies
about how the perfect bride
will be the perfect wife
and live a perfect life.
I adorned myself in jewels
in promises of sweet glittering
magical moments of merriment ahead,
as I covered myself with the perfect
Indian veil.
And as the veil of perfection
cracked to make way for
heart ache,
as I watched my perfect children
shrivel at life's cruel fist . . .
heartache
settled upon souls
like confetti dusts
heartache

from a wedding long dead.

What is left after the wedding day?

A marriage that stands in

the remnants of society's broken lies

picking up the fragments

to piece together

and create a new truth.

So

now I will be a bride again

I wed dark realities

and make love to the shadows

in the absence of the light,

fallen are the facades and falsehoods,

my chuni is frayed,

my bangles have broken,

my henna long gone

but a new vow

arises amidst this deep desperate dance . . .

darling, this broken heart

will dare to dream

dare to love

and dare to be

within the broken pieces.

Woman Divine

They told me women were small.
Weak in our sensitivity and tears,
our touch seduction . . .
They told me Mary Magdalene
was a whore
and that Joan of Arc
was a witch.

I tell you, your tears heal the nations.
Our touch can heal the world.
I tell you Mary Magalene
was divine
and Joan of Arc, powerful.

You see, those who don't understand
the power of the
divine feminine
are afraid of our power.
They had you believing you
were small all your life.

I tell you,
you were never small.
You are powerful,
divine,
a force.

Rise up
and meet
yourself.

Divinity Caged

She was caged and repressed,
my feminine divine
and put in a box
with handcuffs and twine.
Patriarchy repressed me,
society preached . . .
I am bruised, I am broken,
I am wild and I am free . . .

I burned through the twine
and cut every chain . . .
Let there be ashes,
transformation is gained.
Never to be suffocated
or forced to play small
because your lust has no dignity,
and your penis no balls.

Goddess

Inspired by Andrea Thompson's spoken word poem
The Strength of a Woman

Singing Shakti, Shanti
Shakti, Shanti

And upon her head a crown was placed . . .
born of roses, pierced by thorns
her breath had transformed into fire
her soul lighting
her heart thunder.

Her eyes were made of Kali
her thighs drenched with lust
her spirit consumed by Oya
her blood driven by Aphrodite.

Earthly yet divine, divine yet earthly
she confuses men with her desire
makes them weep in her embrace
comforts them through strength in suffering
yet consumes them with peace.

Weeping in her web of danger
and destruction
yet engulfed in her enigma of
charismatic creation.

Singing Shakti, Shanti
Shakti, Shanti

She's a walking oxymoron
of beautiful destruction
and orgasmic peace
leaving you at her altar
on your knees
compelling worship.

Singing Shakti, Shanti
Shakti, Shanti,
Ommmmmm . . .

Duality of Kali Ma

Passion flows
beneath her breasts.
Life undulates
From her breath.

Oh kindred kisses
of Kali Ma's lips,
oh the wrath
of her darkened bliss.

Great mother
of infinite compassion
dueling with demons,
and dancing with passion.

Warrior strength,
and womanly wiles.
Delicate divinity,
and dominion that defiles.

Yours is the light
which strikes hearts with love.
Yours is the power
that shakes darkness with blood.

Yours is the beauty
weeping men mourn,
yours is the strength
that women call home.

I Will Speak

I will speak. I speak
for every woman
that has lost their voice . . .
I will tell their stories
while I hold their hand.

I will sing. I sing
for your inner child
who has lost her songs,
and forgotten the music,
and remind you to dance.

I will dance. I dance
for every woman
who has lost her step
and forgotten her songs.

I will dream. I dream for
every woman
who has sacrificed
their heart and soul
for their loved ones

and forgotten who they are.
I will dream for you.

I will scream. I scream
for every woman who stifles
their pain, I will allow
the pain to surface,
and transform, and be freed.

I will rage. I rage
for every woman
who has lost their spark
and forgotten how to fight,
who have been raped or
beaten or silenced.
I will rage for you sister.
I will rage.

I will rise. I rise
for every woman, mother, sister,
daughter, friend.
I rise for you . . .
Speak, sing, dance, dream, scream, rage
and rise with me.

They Named You Kaur

The mystery is over
truth is revealed
your eyes were always
the open door

The purpose does not
lie in tomorrow
just be with today and
spirit will soar.

Your search is over
answers in the mirror.
You are the one
you have been waiting for.

You were always sacred
always enough
always crowned
so they named you Kaur.

Witch

Witch . . .

take back your power.

When they throw you in the flames

rise like the phoenix

transform in your power.

Rise in the flames of suffering

transcend

become who you were meant to be.

Witch, you were never evil, vulgar, demonic . . .

but healing, beautiful, divine.

They fear the truth

of your power . . .

Reclaim yourself

and be free.

The Witch is Born

Within the broken harmonies
of the symphony of her song,
and the dried up paint
of her unfinished canvas,
on the dusty stage
with lights long gone....
She forgot she existed.

She lost herself,
a poet without a rhyme,
like the clock without time,
a singer without a song,
a lover who does you wrong,
an artist without a brush,
an addict without a rush.

Life had already taken her
through the storms,
then lightning strikes thrice
before the witch is born.

Rebirth is powerful.

The Face of Womanhood

Womanhood resides
in my grandma's skin
where creases tell stories
of where love begins.

Womanhood resides
in my mother's lips
which speak love and hope
with the cha that she sips.

It sparkles wisdom
through my daughter's eyes
for a woman so young
but a soul so wise.

Womanhood's confidence
is in my older sister's chin
held up high
with the strength within.

And the loyalty found
within the scent of sorrow . . .

My ambitious little sister
leaves her heart out to borrow.

And the compassion found
in my best friends' ears
and the laughter that holds me
up through the years.

The face of womanhood
is found within
loving qualities
of women with caramel skin.
Mothers, sisters, daughter and friends . . .

Divine qualities which one peruses . . .
An ode to womanhood, you are my muses.

To the Patriarchy

I speak my opinions,
so call me a bitch.
I stand in my power,
so label me witch.
I will not respond
to your sly advances,
put away your play book,
you've got no chances.

Reduce me to my body
cause you can't handle my mind.
Attach me with strings?
Boy? Are you blind?
Boy, I am fire,
my essence stands tall,
don't pull on strings and
expect me to play small.

No amount of rain
will put out this fire,
your shackles and chains
won't quench my desire . . .

sick of lies
pretending to be small.
I'm not here to serve you,
I'm not your doll.

Your ego's deflated . . .
So call my mind ugly.
Dismiss female power
as you walk away smugly.
Yet the only thing dirty
is your reflection
The only thing defeated
is your erection . . .

Don't like a strong woman,
here is the door . . .
but I won't play the part
of a muted, puppet whore.

Queen

Young Queen,

rise into yourself . . .

You know not who you are.

You have forgotten your beauty,

your power, your magnificence.

My darling, you were never broken . . .

for all is an illusion

and only love real . . .

Rise into yourself young Queen

Rise

Rise

Rise into love . . .

Enough

Not pretty enough.
Not pretty enough.
Put on more lipstick,
botox will do the trick,
buy more stuff.

Not thin enough,
not curvy enough . . .
lose weight,
gain weight,
buy more stuff.

Not smart enough,
too smart, enough!
Patronize me,
ostracize me,
make it tough.

Not sexy enough,
hoe, that's enough . . .

Too pious,
too erotic,
never enough.

Fuck the LIES . . .
ENOUGH!
You are
ENOUGH!

Woman

Woman,
Know your worth?
You are the heart
that gives life
to all.
Why do
you doubt yourself?

Listen
to the words
the heart will
sing . . .
cut the strings.
You are not
a puppet.
And you are
not a doll . . .
not here
to be controlled,
not here for their
amusement . . .
you never were.

Expand your vision
beyond the cage
society created.
Grow wings
and fly.

Sister
Mother
Daughter
Lover . . .
Leave your
strings on the ground
and rise
into yourself.

Make Me Your Doll

Contort my body
into this box of perfection.
Reduce me to the
physical
with lust and seduction.
Reduce me
seduce me
adorn me with strings.
Make me a doll
like beautiful things . . .
force me to play
a part in your drama,
may Kali craft
a piece of your
karma . . .

Savagely ravage my
plastic frame . . .
Stop, I've had enough
of this game!
Women aren't puppets,
Women aren't dolls,

Women aren't mindless,
Women aren't small.
Out of the box
and placed on a shrine,
imperfectly perfect.
Our souls are divine.

Boys Don't Cry

Hush
Boys don't cry
Man up
Keep it inside
Allow that sorrow
to feed your demons instead
Allow it to
coddle your wrath and rage
and increase your suffering.

Hush
Boys don't cry
Man up
Keep your scars inside
where they will
pierce your soul
and drench your heart
in darkness.

Pretend the pain
isn't there
wear a mask

and become the demon
instead.

Because hell forbid
if you cry
and hell forbid
if you heal your wounds instead.

So hush,
Hush,
Hush,
Until your heart is hollow
and your soul
frozen frost to
placate the devil.

The Call of the Wild

Gather, my sisters.
Listen to the call of the wild
the voices whispering within us,
callings from within
the pulsations of heart
and the flow of sacred blood
whispering . . .

Woman,
you are powerful.
Woman,
you are divine.
Woman,
you are everything.
Woman,
you will be fine.
Woman,
hear your heart
and listen to your soul.
The call of the wild lives there.
Do not fear the darkness,
run naked towards the fire . . .
Brave, courageous and bold.

Songs of Darkness

In honor of the 215 Tk'emplups te secwepemc children's bodies found in the Kamloops residential school. In honor of more than 4100 documented burials and missing children of children in residential schools in Canada . . .

To be silent is to be complicit in the secrecy and deception which has dishonored the truth of this genocide for far too long.

The very least we can do in the midst of this horror is to Honor the truth and Honor these lost souls . . . The very least we can do is remember them.

I honor you with my words and prayers that your souls may rest in peace. I will remember you.

Lullaby for the Lost Loves

Go to sleep, child.
Go to sleep.
And let the Creator
hold your head high
in dreams of love
and visions of magic
while you leave
the pains of this world
behind.

Go to sleep, child.
Go to sleep.
The Nation did not
treat you right,
atrocities too dark,
secrets too deep.
So now
you must go to sleep.

Rise, child, rise.
Rise in the light that you are.
Rise in the love

that you deserved
but could not feel
on this earth . . .
until now.

I have not your songs to sing,
I have no right to sing them.
But I can sing mine
if that's ok,
in an Indian lullaby . . .
"*Sooja meray batay*
Thou cahay sohay na
Meeti Meeti lori
Sonahay theri maa . . ."
So
go to sleep, lost loves,
go to sleep.

World Gone Mad

Within the whispers of the wind
there's a place where
illusions end and true love begins ..
elusive and lost in
this world gone mad . . . .

The audacity of assuming that
love is your weapon . . .
when love is always
our ultimate truth
and savior . . .

Lost in a world full of oxymorons
and hyperboles, while visions
dance in your head.
Pulling at strands of reality,
confused with phantom philosophies
grasped at in vain
sanguine pain,
love that is war
madness that feels sane.

Speak to me, then, of
truth in this madness,
remind me of
divine intention
before the insanity
of this illusion
pulls me too deep,
where Angels weep
and peace kisses pain
and leaves me insane
drowning in
phantom philosophies.

Save me from
this enigma of
paradoxical pain in paradise
in this world gone mad.

My Very Last Prayer

These crumbling walls,
these insidious layers,
where suffering crawls,
no room for prayers . . .
Where the beast resides,
the Angels cry.
Here I sit.
Here I'll die.

Here I sit, and here I cry.
Here I plead, here I'll die.
Here I'm frozen, here I'm shook . . .
Salacious suffering with just one look.
These crumbling walls,
these insidious layers,
where suffering crawls . . .
no room for prayers.

Where are you, then . . .
my loving God?
Where is the light?
Or art though fraud?

Is this life
or is this sin . . .
When will hope
and joy begin?

I wait for answers,
I plead for truth,
I kneel before you,
Why so aloof?
These crumbling walls,
these insidious layers . . .
Suffering silenced
my very last prayer.

Where Darkness is Friend

She dances amongst demons
that pretend to be gods,
parades amongst shadows
deceitful and fraud
betrayed by lovers
behind shaded masks
drank of the blood
not wine, in the flasks . . .
She walks barefoot
across winters sand
soul echoing a torture
at betrayal's hand.
The veils are so thick,
illusion, deceit.
The lies are concrete
amongst bloodied feet.
So she walks blind
and dances in pain,
amongst shadows and demons
guilt and shame.

Dancing in circles
that don't seem to end . . .
Where light is forsaken
and darkness is friend.

Where Demons Hark

Midnight hallucinations
delusions of dark
mysterious mists
and foreign fogs.
Kiss of unreason
breath untamed,
demented mind
where love
has no name.

A blood stained epitaph
. . . all that remains,
where life bled bitterly,
and the suffering stains.
Midnight hallucinations
delusions of dark
where love
has no name
'tis where demons
Hark.

Death of a Dream

Tap Tap Tap . . .
Do you hear it?
There's a knock
but there's no door.

Tap Tap Tap . . .
It's coming
from beneath the earth.

Do you hear her?
Whispering lamentations through the ground?
She's lost, she's buried, her soul
is aching and calling out.

Hushhhhhh now
be very quiet
or you won't hear her
crying, helpless, wondering why she was buried.

Her woeful whispers carried by the wind
don't know where she ends, or where she begins . . .
The breath of hope buried and pleading into the night,

knocking with ice cold fingers,
begging your icy heart.

Will you unbury her?
Will you love her?
Will you hold her in your arms,
caress her, be gentle with her grief,
kiss her lips, reassure her, reignite her passion?

Tap Tap Tap
She's knocking at your grave . . .
It's your dream.

Land of Shadows

I have been to the
land of shadows . . .
looking for the light
where I found only darkness.

Cold indifference
piercing ice to the heart
frozen souls
hollow hearts
vast emptiness
lonely roads
leading to the desert of shame
and the oceans of sorrow . . .

Where the lamenting cry,
abominations ruminate on anguish
and screams pierce through the core.

Beware the shadows
set them free
before you become lost
in their world
and forget yourself.

Mirror for Monsters

There's a mirror for monsters
reflecting the truth of you
as you stab me in the back
while holding my hand.
And even as I watch
reflections of my blood stained back
the antidote to your poison
lies closer than you know
within my own heart
in a magic, a potion called love.

So unveil the beast, my love,
unleash the wild
untether the savage storm
to cleanse my sorrows
and wash away
the blood of betrayal . . .
for within myself
dichotomy
divinity amongst darkness,
lies love,
my salve,

my salvation,
my sustenance,
my reflection . . .
my forever home.

And be not afraid my love
as sometimes the
mirror for monsters
unveils your own reflection.

You are your own hero,
you are your own foe.

Could Wrath be an Angel

Could wrath be an angel
wrapped in midnight wings?
An angel full of fury . . .
An angel devoid of glory?

Should praise be bestowed
upon her piercing gaze?
Could she contain wisdom
deep beneath her craze?

Could there be a lesson
hidden within her grasps?
of humility . . .
of acceptance . . .
to change or to clasp?

Stop fighting her grasp
or her claws will leave blood . . .
Stop pushing and shoving,
bathe in the mud . . .
Succumb to her passion,
make love to her wings.

learn her song

and suffering shall sing . . .

Sing songs of anger,

dance on the edge.

Dance with the danger.

Dance on the ledge.

Accept your darkness

and watch the dark wings fly home.

Lay Down Your Hatred

There's a demon in Heaven
and Hell in our hearts
sin found the saint
and tore her apart.

Reason is madness
and madness prevails.
Mercy was lost
long ago set her sails.

The masked knights are pirates
in search of your treasure.
The crowned queen is laughing,
your pain is her pleasure.

The devil laughs,
the angel cries.
The impoverished take arms,
the saint dies.

Hatred's a cloak
so heavy, it's anguish.

Peace is buried
so deep she will languish.

The demon is in Heaven
when Hell is in our hearts.
Lay down your hatred,
excavate peace, and start . . .

The Shadow

Beware the darkness
that creeps into your head . . .
The slow moving shadow,
so quiet you can not hear its breath.
Seeping into your blood so slowly,
you won't know where you start or it ends.
Slowly permeating your body,
and saturating your soul
until you are drowning in the darkness,
suffocating in sacrifice,
shunned in the shade.

Is it coming, or is it going?
Is it stagnant, or is it flowing?
Is it madness, or is it melody?
Like an earnest, eager elegy?
It does not reason, it does not rhyme.
It is not mindful, it deludes time.
It is not a friend, it is a foe . . .
You can't race with it, you must slow . . .

Breathe and be, breathe and be,

sit still with the darkness . . .

sit quietly . . .

listen with your heart, listen with your soul . . .

and you can hear it breathing . . .

Amongst the whispers of your own powerful light.

Illuminate the love, illuminate the love . . .

the shadow

Has no power in love's might.

The Serpents Smile

The children are singing
and playing their games.
Butterflies dance
in the wake of the day.
Cotton candy kisses
pleasing the tongue,
innocence enchants
the minds of the young . . .

Amidst the songs
the day turns cold,
the butterflies die,
the candy turns old.
And in the darkness
a grueling laugh . . .
slaughtering innocence
along the path.

Beware the betrayal
of the serpent's smile.
She laughs, she sings
and stings awhile.

Never truthful,
never to stay,
only to deceive
the light of day.

Oscillating

Waiting
Waiting
Oscillating
between darkness
and light.
Between suffering
and joy
day
and night.

If only
I could hold onto
the sunshine
and bring it
into your darkness
and light it
on fire.

If only
I could encapsulate
the warmth
and thaw

icy hearts,

delusions of mind,

and spark your very soul.

If only

I could be one

with your suffering

kiss its icy lips

until it melts away

into oblivion

leaving love

in its wake.

If only

If only

If only I could heal your heart

if my own heart

wasn't shattered

while I sit here retrieving its pieces

but it's too dark to see them

here in the darkness

as I sit

Waiting

Waiting

Oscillating

between night

and day.

The Broken Place

Shattered windows,
skewed perspectives . . .
broken dreams
and hope defective . . .
the sun won't shine
the words don't rhyme,
the blind will follow
'til the end of time.

Where ghosts will
haunt
the
hallowed hearts . . .
where light will end,
where darkness starts.
Meet me there
at the broken place.
Meet me there
with grief's embrace.

We will not laugh
we dare not smile

in sin we dance
and wait awhile.
For the window
shattered,
the dream
is gone.
All that mattered
now
ashes beyond.

So dance with me
in rooms of dark,
sing with me
with wretched hearts.
Meet me there
with grief's embrace.
You're not alone
in the broken place.

The World of Words

The world of words
where darkness seeps
into the broken cracks of the fragile mind
perseverations
creating hell
screams of anguish . . .
crimson shadows
where demons dwell
and scoff at the suffering of souls
suffocating
breathless
no air
trapped in crimson
hell, rage, fire, blood
eyes too red to see
heart seething
walls closing in
and at the edge of madness he shouts,
"You're worthless!
You've ruined my life!
I hate you."

The world of words
breathing deeply
where
presence sets the captive mind free
where
the aroma of coffee stirs the sleepy eyes awake
to finally truly seek magic
eyes wide open now
where butterflies flutter in open spaces
ears finally listening now
to melodies that produce magic
and ocean waves cleanse the soul
with one simple sound
where even the darkened skies
glisten with star light
and at the edge she stands
where Heaven entices her wings to open
free
from the edge of nirvana she sings,
"I love you.
You are everything
and more."

Words are powerful
destruction
or creation
chose wisely.

Blood Ink

Blood ink
tells the tales
deep within my veins.
Blood that flows
onto the page
and marks the poem
in crimson shades.
Bleeding stories
into formation
Bleeding words
into creation.
Bleeding veins
empty of humanity
crossing over
into divinity.

Dark Angel,
Dark Angel . . .
do not forsake
these wicked hands
guided by darkness
this shallow mind

confined by mortal
idolatry and limitations
this soul chained
into oblivion . . .
Dark Angel
take pity
and set me free
beyond humanity's reach
immortalize me
in love,
for a fool I was
once
a fool I was twice,
a fool that was searching
in vain for the sustenance
found only
in blood ink
metamorphosized
into an offering,
a sacrifice
secured in sacred secrets,
a prayer, a plea for
paradoxical praise
amidst punishment . . .
before my humanity
bleeds me dry . . .
let your dark wings
be my savior.

Reborn

I made love to the darkness,
tangled myself in his lifeless limbs,
danced to his mad melody
of melancholic mania,
kissed the icy lips of his frozen soul
and allowed the breath to penetrate my light
as I succumbed to his night,
surrendered to all seductive suffering
whilst wrapped in a wintry wrath . . .
he consumed me
he buried me whole.

Only then could I be reborn
into the light.

Songs of Love

Love is Who I Am

"You'll regret loving me"
said the snake to the dove . . .
"I sting by nature,
I know not how to love.
I dwell in the fire
lust is my game.
You'll regret loving me,
you will burn in the flames."

"But love is my nature,"
said the dove to the snake.
Love is who I am,
I will never forsake.
So sting if you must,
devour me in flames.
Reduce me to ashes
and bathe me in shame.
But I will not regret,
for blind are the damned.
I am forged in the fire,
and Love is who I am."

Space for Me

I will hold a space for you . . .
Will you hold a space for me?
Space to laugh,
space to dream,
space to love
and just be me?

I will hold a space for you . . .
Will you hold a space for me?
See my soul,
desire my heart?
Take our broken pieces
and create art?

I'll see you,
will you see me?
I'll see your light
if you let me shine.
If you need a heart
you can have mine.

I'll hold you,
can you hold me?
And dream my dreams
and be my wings?
Because in the dark world
I'll help you see . . .

So will you hold
a space for me?

Sword of Love

If only I could take
sunshine
and capture it in a jar,
soothe your scathed soul,
no matter how far.
If only I could
bottle up my tears
to quench your parched heart
and drown all your fears.

Can I step into your darkness
my love,
and light it with my flames?
Can I kill the beasts,
my love
so silence befalls their names?

Can I slay the terror
with a sword of love?
Can I seduce the demons
with kisses of the dove?

For all the light the sun may hold,

and every tear collected . . .

For every fire that I have lit,

and every weapon selected . . .

Will it be enough,

my love?

Or will I sit neglected?

I will continue trying

my love,

until Heaven on earth is perfected.

Self Love

She was so busy loving others,

she forgot to love herself . . .

She poured from her own glass

until it was near empty.

She gave of herself

until her chest felt hollow . . .

She cried for others

and had no tears left for herself.

Her garden grew weeds

whilst she had grown flowers for others.

And when the final storm came

she was drenched in the rainstorm,

on her knees,

begging for a miracle.

And a strange thing happened.

The rains filled her glass,

refilled her tears,

healed her heart,

and fertilized the garden . . .

Then the rainbow came,
and the sun shone
and she smiled
with love
for herself.

I Rise in Love

I had fallen into the dark and dangerous abyss,
stumbled into the pit of salacious suffering.
The flames of Hell I had thrice kissed,
whilst I heard the demons dance and sing . . .
And yet, it's true, I rise.
I have felt the senseless serpent sting,
I have bled from the blade of sacrifice.
I have counted for naught with hopeful eyes,
consumed all of fire, felt frozen in ice.
and yet, for love, I rise . . .

I have thanked the Heavens when all was Hell,
drowned my demons amidst desperate pleas,
prayed in silence upon deaf ears.
And yet in the darkness, I still decree . . .
that yet I rise,
I rise, I rise,
in love.

Always Divine

My love . . .
Why do you hide
behind falsehood,
glitz,
glamour,
makeup,
and think you have to put on your pretty?
Why do you aspire
for recognition,
accolades, praise,
in order to feel worthy?

Why do you feel
invisible
and unseen?

Don't you know?
Your heart is your beauty,
your soul is your worth,
you are always seen.

All else is superficial,

though pleasing to ego . . .

and that's ok.

We have come

to be human,

after all.

To play,

to love,

to fly in freedom.

Just don't forget

in the midst of this stage

that

you are always enough,

always loved,

always seen,

always divine.

This Little Heart

This little heart
is
weathered and worn,
used, abused,
beaten and torn . . .
but don't worry darling,
for I know this to be true,
for the more love is given
it comes back too.

So though
hearts be
weathered
broken and torn,
remember in darkness
light is reborn.

Just Love

Slaves to our mind
chained to our stories
confined by our thinking
but our hearts can set us free . . .

Prisoners of our own creation,
perpetuating our own demise,
blinded by the character we created,
veiled to the truth of love.

So love then . . . And lift the veil.
Love, then . . . deconstruct the illusion.
Love, then . . . Break your chains . . .
Love, just love, just love.

Love Letter

If I could capture the call of the bird,
the sounds of the brook,
the cool crisp breeze cleansing my lungs,
I'd bottle it up as a gift for you.
I don't have a bottle,
will a pen do?
My pen will encapsulate it into a love letter
and you shall feel the breath
of my dawn through my words
and her songs of joy
and sighs of sorrow
on the rise of another morrow.

Dance With Me

Dance with me
and don't let go . . .
Although the tune
is awkward and slow . . .
Though you step on my feet
and bruise my heart,
dance with me love,
and don't ever part.

Dance with me,
and don't let go . . .
although we stumble,
and suffer . . . we grow.
Though the toast became
but shattered glass,
our bloodied feet
will continue to dance.

So dance with me, love
together we pray
to make sense of
all the chaos one day.

And though it was painful
it was also perchance
the most lovely, most beautiful
and Heavenly dance.

She Was Love all Along

She buried the truth
so deep in her garden
that no one could find it.
Then she forgot about it
and it rained,
it stormed,
it hailed,
it burned.
One day
above the cinched and
weathered soil
a tiny rose sprouted
and eventually bloomed.
And she remembered
her truth
that was buried . . .
She was love all along.
She was love all along.
She was always always
love all along.

Love Love Love

Embedded in the fabric of our society
blatant lies
curse the ears that listen
of their unworthiness.

Woven into the minds is madness
dark tales of woe
implicate lost souls
indoctrinated
with propaganda.

Braided is corruption
interlaced in cultural
etiquette
parading as paradise
yet blinded in fog
compromised is the vision
of all who fail to see
through the veil of
illusion and deceit.

When will you hear?

When will you see?

When will you think?

When will you be?

Who are you truly?

Beyond fabrication . . .

Beyond material passion . . .

lust and elation?

Thrice rise

into your simple

powerful truth . . .

Love.

Love.

Love.

Before You Die

Bathe
in the light
before
you kiss
the darkness.

Spread
your wings
before
you jump
from the ledge.

Sing
a song
before
you face
the storm.

Dance
with Angels
before

you embrace
suffering.

Love
before
you die.

I See You

I see you . . .
I see how hard you try
not to allow that darkness to
overtake you.
Do you see me too?

I feel you . . .
I feel the love and kindness
emanating from your heart
and spirit,
spreading joy.
Do you feel me?

I know you . . .
I know you are love
and loved.
I know your darkness
but more importantly
I know your light.
Do you know mine?

I see you.

I feel you.

I know you.

I love you.

So it's okay if you don't . . .

As long as you remember

that I will always see you.

Freedom

Freedom is the choice
in the midst of great suffering,
to love instead of hate,
to hope instead of fear,
to laugh instead of rage,
to accept instead of resist,
to surrender into serenity
and be . . .
when we make the choice to step out
of great darkness
and allow ourselves to feel great light
we grow invisible wings
and fly.

A Force

He mistook her kindness for weakness.

That was when she rose

with eyes full of fire

and songs full of mirth

and a heart infused with love.

This same compassion that

she showed to others,

she had learned to show herself.

He hesitated . . .

He hadn't known

she was a different kind of fire . . .

she was a different kind of love . . .

she was a different kind of song.

The way she fought for others,

she had finally learned

to requite in love for herself,

and that was a force

to be reckoned with.

The Ultimate Victory

Weary of warrior songs,
battered by battles with no beginning
and no end,
the forever fighter saunters
in submission to the fire,
in surrender to the fight.

She places her sword
amidst the fury of the blaze
and surrenders her armor
into the flames.

And as she succumbs to suffering sublime,
a paradox of pain and perfection,
an oxymoron of
torture and transcendence,
as dusk turns
into the deepest night,
her soul
transforms into
a magical reverie of
firefly hopes

lighting the sky
ablaze in love . . .
the ultimate victory.

Songs of Home

Gypsy No More

She's a gypsy,
her heart has no home.
Abroad she searches, and wanders,
and walks and walks and walks.
She walks through deserts, scorned by scorching
sunlit skies
and fields of ice leaving blue icy lips and frozen hearts
and forests of dead end dreams and dismal drudgery,
deafening cries of the dead . . .
Still she walks and walks and walks . . .

She comes upon a fork in the path.
Upon her two chalices were placed,
one of wine so sweet it teased the tongue,
the other of blood sacrifice so somber . . .
she was asked to choose.
The first path was lit by a golden sun
butterflies and flowers and songs of love and bliss.
The second path was dreary,
the sun refused to shine, she would have to hold her own light . . .
She would have to sing her own songs, and plant her own flowers,
and shine her own light.

And in the darkness she saw the childrens' eyes
pleading for her to shine her light,
yearning for her flowers,
begging for her songs.

Her heart guides her home
to her own light,
a gypsy no more.

Whisperings

When the whisperings fade away
though the whole worlds dead asleep
when masks are set aside . . .
who am I to be?

When the voices can not speak
to tell me who to be-
lost without my roles . . .
what reflection will I see?

I beckon for time to stand still,
and yearn to see my hearts truth . . .
and listen to my souls song,
tell me, what will be the tune?

What good are these broken wings?
Maimed and grounded, I will pray,
Pray to heal these broken wings, and
fly home one day.

Naked

I want to stand
in the truth of me.
Be naked
vulnerable
raw.

I want to wear less.
Remove this burden of chains
from my shoulders,
remove this aching grief
from my heart.
Heal my bleeding wounds
and patch them with the
medicine of love.

I want to be naked.
I want to wear less.
Wear less worry
less anger
less grief
less sadness
less worldly bullshit

that lies to me and tells me who I should be,

who you should be,

and keep us chained

in a cell

that we can't even see.

I want to fucking burn the

chains, the cell,

the ludicrous ideology

that doesn't serve me.

I want to light a bonfire

for the deception

that keeps us small

and come back from the flames

larger than life,

lighter and naked,

vulnerable and real,

powerful

and free.

I want to stand

in the truth of me.

At My Own Door

Tap tap tapping at my heart
to awaken.
Knock knock knocking
at the door.
Softly whispering
at your window.
Deeply breathing,
pleading
for more.

For all of
the angst
this world has shown me,
for all of the sorrow
that entered my soul.
You were the reason,
Love, Golden Angel.
In the deepest darkness,
you were my star.

The search was futile,
the path never ending,

I was looking above
but the key was below.
So
I'm tap tap tapping at my heart
to awaken.
I'm knock knock knocking
at my own door.

My Soul Wants to Play

My soul wants to play
and laugh in the dark
whilst grasping for fireflies
to keep her warm.

My soul wants to dance
in the storms and the lightning
and transform in electricity
whilst others conform.

My soul wants to dare
daughters to dream,
earth angels to fly
into the heart of the storm.

With laughter, with daring,
with dancing and grace,
with love's vast embrace,
my soul wants to play.

My *Nani's* Hands

My *nani's* hands
were not soft like her heart . . .
They were withered by storms
with much wisdom to impart.

My *nani's* eyes
were kind with compassion,
and spoke volumes of her days
where family was passion.

Within the creases of her skin
were stories of loss and sorrow,
and yet she held her chin up high
her sights set for tomorrow.

Within smells of cinnamon,
and *cha* tasting of cloves,
she took rest upon a weary day,
while watching the harvest grow.

And while in body, she was a farmer,
in spirit a warrior grew.

And due to her warrior spirit,
her *soni chiree* flew.

She flew to new heights, saw new land,
where education was possible.
All due to the withered hands
who had made such dreams plausible.

So should I ever lose my way,
and forget to understand . . .
remind me that love, connection, and, freedom,
are the legacies of my *nanis* hands.

Mirror

Etymology of mirror . . .
Latin *mirare*
to look at
old French *mirour*
to look at
look at
look at yourself
in the mirror
reflections of
benevolence
or
malevolence . . .
Who will you be?
Who will you see?
Are you lost
in your shadows,
do you rise
in your light?
Mortal choices
within the
mirror of meaning . . .

Dichotomies of
divinity amidst humanity . . .
yin and yang . . .
Chained, confined, weak?
Or strong, sovereign and free?
Etymology
of yourself . . .
Look
look
look
and
choose before the mirror,
before they choose for you.

This is Not a Poem

These are not words,

this is the breath from my soul

painting onto the page . . .

infinite stories of joy, sadness, and rage.

This is not a poem,

it's my heart held out to you . . .

beating outside of my body in vulnerable truth

in the hopes that you will hold your heart out too.

These are not just my stories,

they are now yours too . . .

to soothe you, coddle you, stifle you with their pain . . .

Will you listen then?

Will you allow our collective stories,

our collective pain, to become art?

Will you breathe with me? Will you enter my soul?

Will you hold my heart gently and stop it from bleeding?

Because these are not my words . . .

it is the breath from my soul.

This is not my poem, it is my heart held out to you.

This is no longer my story, it is ours.

Who Am I?

Who am I?
Where do I begin?
Raven eyes
and darkened skin . . .
But who am I
beyond this skin?
A heart that beats
a soul that sins?
A pulse that flows
and wished to fly?
But grounded now
she wished to die . . .
Wings were clipped
but soul was kissed.
Who am I then?

Who am I then?
beyond my skin?
Where does hope
and love begin?

All my life
sat in a box
allowed lids to shut
my heart to lock.
I'm tired now,
just want to sleep,
just need some rest,
so my heart can beat . . .
so my blood can flow
and my wings can fly
my mind can dream
and my soul can cry . . .

Who am I then?
Sister, friend?
Mother, lover?
Time just ends . . .
For now I'm buried
in a veil of spells,
thickening illusion,
darkness, Hell.

Lies, more lies
so much deceit.
Ego, delusions,
but never defeat . . .

Because I'm not my eyes,

I'm not my skin,

I'm not my sorrow,

I'm not my sin.

I am love

so powerful . . .

I'm not my body,

I am my soul.

Letter for My Son

We live in a world that can not understand or tolerate differences:

differences of skin,

differences of tongues,

differences of mind . . .

and then I had you . . . my son . . .

different,

different . . .

In the words of Temple Grandin,

different, not less . . .

And son, you are not less than anyone.

just because your brain is different.

Just because at 3 they said you have Pervasive Developmental
    Disorder, not otherwise specified,

now just described as autism.

Just because you could not talk until you were four,

or play with other children . . .

just because you've went to every therapy we could think of . . .

ABA, OT, SLP, music, naturopath, gluten free, dairy free, brain scans,
    supplements, medication, medication, medication.

Just because our thoughts ruminated . . .

thinking . . . Autism, autism, autism . . .

What does it even mean?

Redefining the narrative in our head . . .

University? Maybe not . . . college perhaps?? No, not with
   an intellectual disability . . .

School?

You were kicked out of school at 6

because the school and the world weren't ready for you.

Because the world is too shallow

to comprehend souls that are so deep,

and too boxed to understand

energy that is angelic and free . . .

Not less, never less.

Always more.

And something more was going on,

by 11, your depression so extreme

that you would bolt out of the house

and there was that time

that your depression raged out of control,

you tried to hit your head into the pavement . . .

and the neighbor tried to help and stop you,

and a nervous laugh escaped from my own lips . . .

and the neighbor cried

and he said

"I can't believe how strong you are,

I can't believe you're laughing."

But even through the laughter, though my heart was breaking,

I understood something

that the neighbor didn't . . . that was that

even then, you were never less,

just different.

And I understood that souls like yours come to teach lessons

so profound

but the blind will never see

and the deaf will never hear

that you are here to teach me

love that is

unconditional.

So if they ever say you are less,

remember my words . . .

you are special,

you don't need to sit in anyone else's box or definition of who
you should be . . .

You are worthy because of your soul son . . .

and you will always be worthy because of your magnificent soul

so deep that a shallow world can never process,

so beautiful that small hearts will never understand,

so angelic and free, you have wings to fly

in unconditional love.

Always different, never less.

Love, Mom

Letter for My Daughter

My girl . . .

my heart warrior,

where do I begin? We had no idea that at 11 you would be diagnosed

with a disorder so rare, that it matches the rarity of your soul . . .

because the beauty of your soul has no limits . . .

and so when you inject yourself with a daily dose of hormones,

I hope you remember your beautiful soul calls upon others
to inject themselves too . . .

with a daily dose of kindness, of strength, of courage, of resilience . . .

because your rare condition is a reminder of the rare warrior spirit
that resides in your body,

and your beautiful heart knows no bounds.

Perhaps that is why your aorta was too big for your body

and that is why they needed to do

open heart surgery at 15 . . .

and that scar . . . when you look at it, remember you are beautiful.

It is the scar of a warrior.

It is the scar of a heart that was too big

in a world that can not understand the beauty of love so expansive

or resilience so powerful.

So nothing is wrong with you, my dear . . .

Your scar is your badge and reminder

that hearts filled with such warmth will always find difficulty in a world that is too cold,

yet it is these very hearts

that will melt the icy souls

and propel the world forward,

with the courage of a lion

in a world full of mice

and the compassion of an Angel

in a world full of mortals.

Darling, remind them that we are love . . .

because

you are love

you are loved

you are

always my beautiful heart warrior.

Love, Mom

Listen

Shhhhh...

Do you hear it?

it's a whisper

coming from the unknown...

drowned again

by the vulgar dense darkness of the world...

urging you to just listen...

Listen...

Listen.

Shhhhhhhhh...

do you hear it now?

Contradicting the vulgarity of your mind,

reinforcing the purity of your soul,

knocking at your heart to open,

begging for you to awaken,

remember,

see through the illusion

into truth.

Listen...

it's whispering

whispering hope

whispering faith

whispering love

guiding you back home . . .

if only

if only

if only you would just listen.

More Songs for the Soul

Sing Me a Song

Sing me a song
with melodies of magic,
soothe my soul
of stories too tragic.

Write me a poem
of power and peace,
penetrate my heart
with provocative praise.

Paint me a picture
to place in my home,
mix colors of madness
make music my throne.

Heal my heart
of torment too tragic,
sing me a song
with melodies of magic.

Aching Are the Lustful

She fills the void
with diamonds and pearls . . .
hoping their shimmer
will rub off
on the ache in her soul . . .
but to no avail.

He fills the emptiness
with salacious passions . . .
hoping this will
be the one
that feels like home
but fails.

They bury themselves
in work and pleasure
thinking this will
make them forget
darkness and dejection . . .
life assails.

For
blind are the greedy,
aching are the lustful,
cogs in a system,
mad and meaningless
forever waiting
for their ship
to sail.

Halt, and listen,
halt, and be . . .
the ship
is the destination,
life is the sea . . .
the treasure
was always within
your reach,
look in your heart
and finally see.

Lust

Drenched in ego, losing my name,
burning in passion's fiery flames.
Dancing in dreams of desire . . .
falling recklessly into the fire.
Robbed of romance and innocent musings,
into the pit of salacious suffering.

Hark . . .
in the place that the Angels sing.
Ache in the despair the demon brings.
Mystery unfolds and reason beguiled,
beware the songs of the sirens' wiles.

Hark . . .
for the flame of lust knows no bounds,
engulfing the soul without a sound.
Whispering of devious and devilish things,
oh the despair the demon brings.

Hark . . .

the songs of the Angels once more.

Remember your name and your spirit shall soar.

Step away from the fire, away from the night,

into the purity of love and light.

My Heart Told Me to Grieve

My heart told me to grieve today,
upon a winter's eve.
My heart told me to believe today
and falsehoods took their leave.

All that was left today
was sadness dancing with sorrow.
Into the darkness they played
the music into the morrow.

A veil of grief cried misty tears,
a baptism for the soul.
A golden light replaced the place
where grief had left a hole.

My heart told me to grieve today,
upon a winter's eve.
My heart told me to believe today
and falsehoods took their leave.

Forgiveness

She had been carrying
the chains for a while . . .
wearing them on her shoulders
like skin on her bones,
clinging to her life force
diminishing her light
punishing herself for her humanity.
Admonishing herself
for things out of her control . . .
until
she finally broke the chains.
She forgave herself
and grew wings to fly.

Passion

Passion is more
than the meeting of skin . . .
It's where bodies end
and souls begin . . .

Passion is more
than a kiss of desire,
it's the tender heart
ablaze with fire . . .
It is where the earth
kisses the sky,
and demons repent
while the Angels' sigh . . .

It's the melding of bodies
hearts, minds and souls,
it's tasting a dream,
not just living a goal.

So do not mistaken for
it would be a sin
for lust is but hollow
where passion begins.

Light the World on Fire

The flames of passion rise high
and light the world on fire
flaming tongues, piercing lungs
songs of hope and dreams begun . . .
strength in fire
and power in love
shattering the darkness
dancing with doves.
Demons and darkness
fail to conspire
when passion burns,
light the world on fire.

Intimacy

Intimacy is more
than physical touch . . .
it's a melding of minds
singing of souls
healing of hearts.

It is
when you give your heart
away whole
with no expectations
only hopes
that they will keep
your heart safe.

Intimacy is
a
magical
union
of
light.

The Winds of Change

The winds of change have come,
ease into the discomfort.
Allow the storm to become a breeze.
Allow breath to dance in her own rhythms
pulsating like a Latin Lover,
undulating like a belly dancer's navel,
softening into a gentle wave.
Allow your breath to dance
your heart to breathe
and the sun's rays to
kiss your soul free.

Presence

Presence
allows divinity to speak words of wisdom
transforming ordinary moments
into magical, mystical, miraculous music
for the soul . . .

If only we knew how to listen.

And the Music Played

She danced in rain storms
while all watched and whispered
at her foolishness.
"Why doesn't she wait for
the rains to stop
before she dances?"
And the music played.

She danced during the hot spell
while all watched and whispered
at her foolishness.
"Why doesn't she wait
for the sun to set
before she dances?"
And the music played.

She danced during the night
and again they watched and whispered
at her foolishness.

"Why doesn't she wait
for the sun to rise
before she dances?"
And the music played.

Then the sun rose and they were finally ready to dance . . .
And the music stopped.

Heaven's Embrace

When the sunshine kissed my face,
the cool breeze teased my hair.
Passion danced with butterfly wings,
breath was life and love was air.

Pulsations of heart became my dance
vibrations of love became my song.
Reverberations of magic became everything,
echoes of the Eagle kept me strong.

Listen and love will whisper of freedom,
the courage by which perils are erased,
dance and sing in divinity's light,
wrap yourself in Heaven's embrace.

Heaven's Tears

The hardest thing I've ever done
is to accept the suffering of my children . . .
Tell me then, isn't that what God does
every time we cry?
How much pain has he endured then?
Or is it she?

For whether you say Divine, God, Waheguru,
Jehovah, Father, Mother, or Allah . . .
We are speaking to the same great energy that is love.
It is the same energy that we put our hopes and wishes into.
It is the same energy that wraps us in invisible wings
of consolation during our greatest grief.

We can't see these wings,
but if you silence yourself,
in the presence of faith,
and listen to your soul
you can feel Divinity's wings.

Whether the pronouns be

He/him

She/her

They/them

Yin and yang

Binary or otherwise . . .

This same Divinity encompasses

everything

and holds us in their magical embrace of love.

In the name of this love,

every time my children cry

I cry . . .

But I believe God cries for us all . . .

That is why it storms,

Heaven's tears.

Paradox

We breathe to live, but forget to really breathe.

We work for freedom, and never are free.

We seek this freedom and yet are confined . . .

Rules, institutions, and pleasure make us blind.

We are spiritual beings yet are trapped in our phones.

We hope to find love, but our hearts turn to stones.

We seek abundance and forget all we have.

We seek intelligence, yet use only half.

We say God doesn't hear us, but have forgotten to pray.

We expect it all, but don't seize the day.

We cloak our bodies to relieve men of lust,

and are nude for a freedom that objectifies us.

Women are not educated for fear that they may think,

eyes are wide open, but forgotten to blink.

So we put on our masks, and rise to our duty . . .

We mutilate our bodies in the name of beauty.

We endure beatings and bruising in the name of love.

We search for this love when it was always in us.

We were running for joy, buy joy chose to walk,

we yearn for silence yet can't stop our talk.

We breathe to live, but forget to really breathe.

We open our eyes wide, but never really see.

For Shahreen

In the silence of an empty room
a shattered heart weeps . . .
In the solace of contemplation,
an essence that reaps.
In the solemn stares of strangers,
unleashed a pain.
In the misery of self pity,
sorrow knows no name.

To your soul I give a kiss.
Your earthly spirit I shall miss.
I'm too unwise to understand.
To your spirit I lend my hand.

And I feel you . . .
in the softness of the wind,
in the glory of the sun,
where the circle begins,
your thoughts are free to roam.
In the smile of a stranger,
in a heart that believes . . .
like an angel,
your soul is free.

True Wealth

Until you can learn to savor the sunshine and dance in her light . . .

listen to the music in the melody of the trees and feel the spirit of the breeze . . .

until you can relish in a moment with a child and delight in their innocence . . .

until you can smile at a stranger and wish them love and light . . .

you can not be rich.

Until you can stop racing with time, and shake her hand in the moment . . .

until you put more value on the love within than the materialism around . . .

until breathing in joy becomes more important than counting your cash . . .

you can not be rich.

True wealth is measured in joy, not dollars . . .

love, not jewelry . . .

peace, not drama . . .

family and friends, not empty aching souls . . .

drop the deceptive, false fabrications

and ascend in the truth of Love.

Heaven is Bleeding

Fly like a butterfly
into the night
and sing a wild song
or two.

Dance like the fire
on a winters day
and warm up a heart
that's blue.

Feel the essence
of invisible wings
allow your passion
to soar.

Lift your spirit
in Loves embrace
right past Heavens
door.

For butterflies dance
in solemn pursuit

and sing the most
sacred of songs,
and passion can fly
beyond the grave
and love . . . it
can never go wrong.

So fly, my love
and sing
and dance
and love like never before . . .
For Heaven is bleeding,
waiting, and pleading
for you to step through
her door.

The Edge of Silence

the edge of silence
where divinity speaks
in silent whispers
to those who will listen

where magic sprinkles
and fairy dust glitters
for dreamers who dare
to see

where lost souls
find their purpose
in strands of
star dust sprinkled
in the spaces
in between
the seconds
that chime between
the clock as time stands still

shhhhhhh . . .
can you listen?

can you open your fucking eyes?

can you just stop and stand still in this moment?

can you breathe?

can you be?

at the edge of silence

Awaken

Sacred waves
undulations of life
prana, chi, light . . .
simple yet cosmic,
miniscule yet profound,
earth bound.

Droplets of rain,
rays of sunshine,
waves in the ocean,
waves in our hearts,
storms in our minds . . .
misery which is kind . . .
and kindness which is miserable.

Blinded by the veil
confused in the chaos
mists of delusion
flames of seduction
tearing apart the physical
until all that's left
is nothing and everything
all at once.

All at one

time stands still

time was never motionary

and it's time

time to scream

and shout

and cry

and laugh and heal

and die.

It's time

time

to become reborn again

until all is nothing

and everything

all at once

rise and awaken

awaken

awaken.